MW00365693

THE USEFUL KNOTS BOOK

HOW TO TIE THE 25+ MOST PRACTICAL ROPE KNOTS

SAM FURY

Illustrated by
DIANA MANGOBA

Copyright SF Nonfiction Books © 2016

www.SFNonfictionBooks.com

All Rights Reserved

No part of this document may be reproduced without written consent from the author.

WARNINGS AND DISCLAIMERS

The information in this publication is made public for reference only.

Neither the author, publisher, nor anyone else involved in the production of this publication is responsible for how the reader uses the information or the result of his/her actions.

CONTENTS

THANKS FOR YOUR PURCHASE

Did you know you can get FREE chapters of any SF Nonfiction Book you want?

https://offers.SFNonfictionBooks.com/Free-Chapters

You will also be among the first to know of FREE review copies, discount offers, bonus content, and more.

Go to:

https://offers.SFNonfictionBooks.com/Free-Chapters

Thanks again for your support.

INTRODUCTION

Anyone can tie "lots of knots", but a proper knot will be stronger and easier to untie. It will also help to conserve rope as you will use less (lots of knots uses more than needed) and having to cut the knots out is less likely since they are easier to untie.

There are many knots, far too many for the average person to remember. Fortunately, there is no need to remember them all. Just being able to tie a handful of knots is enough to see you through any situation when a knot is needed.

The Useful Knots Book is a no-nonsense how-to book on tying the 25+ most useful knots. It comes with easy to follow illustrated instructions and tips on when to best use each knot.

KNOT TYING TERMS

For ease of explanation when describing how to tie knots the following terminology will be used.

Bight

Any bend in-between the ends of the rope which does not cross over itself.

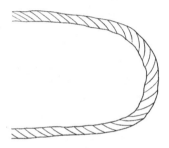

Crossing Point

The point where the rope crosses over itself.

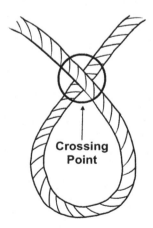

Crossing
Point

Load

Refers to the weight of the object being secured, e.g., if you are pulling a log then the log is the load.

Loop

Similar to a bight but the ends cross over, hence creating a closed circle.

An overhand loop is when the running end lies over the top of the standing part. An underhand loop is opposite (the standing part lies on top of the running end).

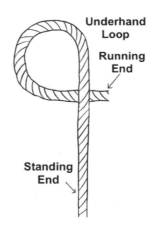

Rope

A generic term used in this book that refers to cord, rope, string, twine, or whatever material which is being used to tie a knot.

Running End

The part of the rope used to tie the knot. Also known as the working end.

Standing End

The part of the rope other than the running end.

Shock Load

Shock load occurs when there is a sudden increase in load. In such a case the load will be much more than the actual weight of the object. An example of this is when a climber falls and his/her weight suddenly loads the rope.

Turn

A single wrap of the rope around an object. A round turn (pictured) is where the object is completely encircled.

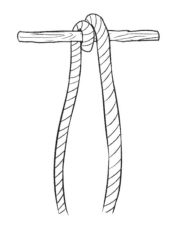

ROPE CARE

Proper rope care will prolong a rope's strength and usability. The same basic rules apply whether you have top quality climbing rope or handmade twine from plant fibers.

Avoiding Deterioration

There are many things that will increase deterioration. When possible, avoid the following:

- Animals. Animals can gnaw and scratch at rope.
- Corrosives. Avoid chlorine, markers, oils, paints, petrol, and all other chemicals and corrosives from coming into contact with rope.
- Dampness. Constant damp conditions weakens the structure of rope.
- Heat. Any extreme and/or prolonged heat damages rope, such as fire or direct sunlight.
- Friction. Friction can heat and cut rope. Note that rope rubbing on rope will cut it.
- Dirt. Dirt can work its way into rope making it stiff and brittle. Avoid leaving rope directly on the ground and be careful of stepping on it.
- Sharp edges. Sharp edges will cut rope. Be careful of glass, metals, rock, etc. Place something between the rope and any sharp edges for protection, e.g., lay carpet over the rock you need to pass the rope over.

Preventing Fraying

This refers to protecting of the ends of the rope. There are basically two ways to prevent fraying.

- Fusing is done by melting the ends.

- Whipping is a method that uses a smaller string to bind the tips of the rope.

Whipping is better than fusing but takes more time. A combination of whipping and fusing is the best.

Simple Whipping Method

There are a few ways to whip a rope. Here is a simple and effective one.

Lay your whipping string along the rope. Wrap it around the rope five to ten times in such a way that the string will hold itself in place.

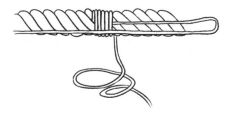

Make a bight with the string and then continue to wrap it around the bight and the rope five to ten times. Thread the end of the string through the bight and then pull the other end so that the bight clamps down to secure the string in place. Trim the ends of the string.

Cleaning

Periodically cleaning rope will prolong its integrity. Hand wash the rope in cold water with mild soap. Rinse the soap out and air dry it. Avoid direct sunlight and do not use any artificial heating source.

Flaking

Flaking is a good way to make the rope ready-to-use as it removes kinks and ensures that it will feed out smoothly.

First, take out any knots.

To flake the rope, find one end and lay it on the ground. Pull the rest of the rope through your loose fist and let it fall to the floor.

Coiling

Coiling rope makes it easy to carry, use, and store. It will prevent it from getting tangled and kinks.

There are several ways to coil rope. Here is a fairly easy method that you can adapt to different lengths, thicknesses, and types of rope.

First flake the rope as previously described.

Hold the end of the flaked rope in your right hand. Use your left hand to wrap the rope around your right elbow and the palm of your right hand.

When you run out of rope, use your left hand to grab the coils together in the center.

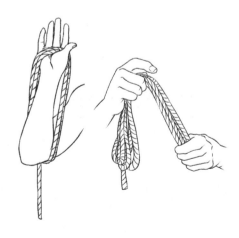

Fold the coils in half and use the loose end of the rope (not the end you held at the start) to wrap tightly around the bunch of coils.

To tie it off, tuck the end of the rope under the last wrap you did and pull it tight.

When you want to use the rope, unravel it in the opposite way, i.e., untie, unwrap, and un-coil. This will prevent tangles.

For shorter rope, wrap it around you hand instead of your hand/elbow.

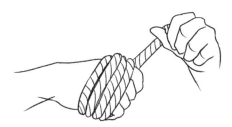

Secure it in the same way. There is no need to fold it in half.

Storage

Once the rope has been coiled either hang it in a cool, dry area or place it in a bag. There are purpose-made rope-bags you can purchase, but almost any bag will do if you don't need something specific, such as a rescue throw bag.

Alternatively, flake the rope straight into the bag and tie the ends to the bag loops so they are easy to locate. This is good for ropes that you need quick access to use, such as rescue ropes.

Inspection and Retirement

Retiring rope means to deem it unsuitable for use. For professionally manufactured ropes the company often gives a recommended usage, but ultimately it is up to you.

For rope that bears weight, especially for critical loads (such as a human), be stricter.

Inspect rope before and after every use. Look for fraying, burn marks, wear and tear, etc.

The rope's history of use is also important to consider. For example, if it has suffered a big shock load, is very old, has been exposed to corrosives, or has been poorly stored, it will be weaker.

Related Chapters:

- Loops

KNOTS

Although in reality you can use any knot any way you wish, most are designed for specific tasks. They are grouped into five broad categories.

For ease of learning, the categories are presented in a progressive manner.

Stopper knots come first because they are often used as a base knot for tying other knots. They are also easier to tie. Next are loops, then hitches, bends, and finally lashing.

Stopper Knots

Stopper knots are useful to add weight to rope, to use as handholds (in a lifeline, for example), to stop rope from slipping through a hole, to stop cut rope from fraying, etc. When tied around the standing end of a rope, they can also be used as a backup to prevent knot failure.

Loops

Loops are usually made by tying the rope to itself to create an enclosed circle. Their main use is as attachment points—as holds to climb up or to clip a carabineer onto, for example.

Hitches

Hitches are useful in securing the rope to an object (a boat to the jetty, for example) or around a log you wish to drag.

Bends

Bends are used to join two or more lengths of rope together. They can be useful in repairing broken rope or for creating a longer length from two shorter ones.

Lashing

Lashing is used to join objects together. It becomes very useful during construction.

CHOOSING THE RIGHT KNOT

All the knots in this book are useful, but there will always be one that's most useful, depending on what you need it for.

To decide which knot to use, you must consider the characteristics of each knot. Gaining in one characteristic will usually mean compromising on another. You must find the knot with the best balance of characteristics for a given job.

Getting the Job Done

You must choose a knot that will fulfill the purpose it is needed for. For instance, a lashing will be more effective in binding two objects together than a a loop knot will.

Security

The security of a knot is its ability to stay tied and tight—that is, not come undone on its own. Constant pressure (or lack of it), thrashing (in the wind or water), vibration, and other movements may compromise the security of a knot.

It will make sense to choose the most secure knot you can, but remember that increasing one characteristic will decrease others. For example, a very secure knot may become very hard to untie, which may be a problem if fast release is a requirement of the job you need it to do.

Strength

Every knot will weaken the integrity of the rope, some more than others. The strength of the knot refers to how much the knot weakens the rope.

When the task at hand (climbing, rescue, or dragging a load, for example) requires the rope to hold weight and/or take shock load, this characteristic becomes important, especially if specialized rope isn't available.

Ease of Tying

When something must be tied quickly or repeatedly, then ease of tying becomes more important. You don't want to spend five minutes tying a knot you have to make more than once.

Ease of Untying

There are circumstances where you may want the knot to be easy to untie, such as if you want to release the knot quickly without cutting the rope.

At other times, you may want the knot to be more difficult to untie, such as when you want to make it difficult for an animal to release itself, or to stop other people from being able to easily untie it.

Another factor is how easy the knot will be to untie after it's done its job. Some knots are designed to be easy to untie even after considerable tension has been applied, or after the rope has swelled underwater, or both.

Related Chapters:

- Lashing

STOPPER KNOTS

Stopper knots are useful to add weight to rope, to use as handholds (in a lifeline, for example), to stop rope from slipping through a hole, to stop cut rope from fraying, etc. When tied around the standing end of a rope, they can also be used as a backup to prevent knot failure.

Overhand Knot

This is the simplest of knots and is the basis of many other knots. An overhand knot is difficult to untie once it's tightened.

Make an underhand loop by taking the running end of the rope and passing it under the standing end. Pass the running end though the loop from the front to the back.

Pull both ends to tighten in.

The overhand knot can be made bulkier by passing the running end through the loop more times. Push the first turn into the middle of the knot.

Doing it twice makes a double overhand, and doing it three or more times creates a blood knot.

Figure-Eight

A figure-eight knot can do all the same things as the overhand knot, but is much easier to untie.

Make an upwards-facing overhand loop, and then make the running end pass back under the standing end. Pass the running end back through the first loop you made. Pull both ends away from each other to tighten the knot.

Quick-Release Figure-Eight

You can make the figure-eight knot quick-release by putting the running end back through the first loop before tightening the knot. To release the knot, pull the running end.

This can also be done with the overhand knot.

LOOPS

Loops are usually made by tying the rope to itself to create an enclosed circle. Their main use is as attachment points—as holds to climb up or to clip a carabineer onto, for example.

Overhand Loop Knot

The overhand knot can also be used to create a loop. It works well with fishing line, but can be hard to untie.

Double up the rope to make a bight, and then tie an overhand knot in the bight.

Bowline

A bowline is a fixed loop that will neither tighten nor slip under strain. It is good to tie around things you want to secure/tether, such as a raft or a person.

Hold the rope in your right hand, with the standing end at the rear. Make an overhand loop so that the loop faces to the left. Pass the running end up through the loop you made and then around the back of standing end.

The running end then goes over the crossing point and back through the original loop.

To tighten the knot, pull the standing end and the doubled-up running end in opposite directions.

You can finish the bowline off with a stopper (overhand) knot tied against the side of the loop.

Once you can tie the bowline, practice doing it around things. It changes the orientation, so practice is needed.

Butterfly Loop

The butterfly loop (a.k.a. alpine butterfly or lineman's loop) is useful for creating a fixed loop in the middle of a rope. It's secure, can be loaded safely in multiple directions, and remains relatively easy to untie even after a heavy load.

Among other things, the butterfly loop is a very good knot to use to shorten a rope or to exclude a damaged section. Doing so is preferable to cutting a rope, since a rejoined rope has less strength.

Get a bight of the rope and twist it twice in the same direction, so you have two crossing points and therefore two loops.

For ease of explanation, the loop furthest away from the ends of the rope will be loop one, and the loop between the ends of the rope and loop one will be called loop two.

Grab the tip of the bight of loop one and bring it beyond the crossing point of loop two.

Next, bring the tip of loop one up through loop two.

Pull all ends to tighten.

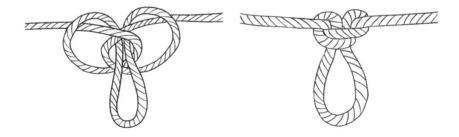

Figure-Eight Loop

Just like the overhand knot, the figure-eight can be turned into a fixed loop by making the knot on the bight.

To tighten it, pull on each loose end—that is, on the loop and the running/standing ends.

Work the knot so it's neat, with no crossover on the rope. This will keep the knot strong and easier to untie.

Threaded Figure-Eight

This is a good way to tie onto a fixed loop. It's often used by climbers, as it's considered more secure than the bowline.

Create a figure-eight in the rope. Be sure to leave a long running end. Pass the running end through/around whatever you want to tie onto, and then use it to trace the path of the original figure 8. Pull it tight in the same way you did the figure 8 loop.

HITCHES

Hitches are useful in securing the rope to an object (a boat to the jetty, for example) or around a log you wish to drag.

Half Hitch

The half hitch is easy to tie and easy to untie even after considerable load. It's designed to take load on the standing end.

Due to its simplicity, it's relatively easy to work loose. To prevent this, the half hitch is usually used in conjunction with other knots. Common examples are the round turn and two half hitches, which use three less secure knots to create one very secure knot that remains easy to tie and untie.

Some common uses for the half hitch on its own are as a backup knot and to use up any leftover rope so it's out of the way.

To tie the half hitch, loop the rope around the object. Bring the running end behind and then back over the standing end. The running end then threads through the loop above the crossing point created.

In this picture, the half hitch is loose, but in actual use it should be pulled tight and repeated (two half hitches) in order to create a more secure knot.

Clinch Knot

The clinch knot is most commonly used as a fishing knot, to tie a hook (or lure, swivel, etc.) to a line. It's best used with lighter lines.

Thread the running end of the line through the eye of the hook, and then do it again in the same direction to create a round turn. Wrap the running end around the standing part at least four times, and preferably more. Holding the loops under your fingers as you do the wraps may make it easier.

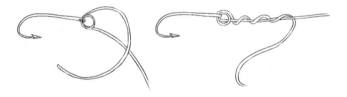

Thread the running end through the loops created by the round turn. This creates a second, bigger loop. Thread the running end down through this second loop.

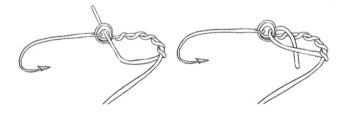

Tighten the knot. The wraps will change position and squash up against the eye of the hook. Trim the end of the running end if needed.

Clove Hitch

Clove hitches are a useful base for many other knots (such as lashing) and are also good for binding in their own right.

Clove hitch method one: When the rope is not under strain as you're tying it, and you're able to slip it over your object, you can use this quick method.

Make two loops in the rope which face opposite directions, as pictured below. Put the right loop over the left one. Put both loops over the object, and then pull the running and standing ends apart to tighten the knot.

Clove hitch method two: Wrap the running end of the rope around the object you wish to tie onto, so that the running end crosses over the standing end. Wrap the running end around a second time, and then pass it underneath itself. Pull it tight as before.

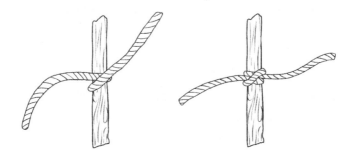

Constrictor Knot

By making a small adjustment in the way you tie the clove hitch, you can create the constrictor knot.

Tie the clove hitch as in method two, but this time, pass the running end underneath the first turn before pulling it tight.

The constrictor knot is good to use when working with thin rope. It's considered more secure than the clove hitch, but is harder to untie.

Cow Hitch

The cow hitch (a.k.a. lark's head) is not a very secure knot, but it is quick to tie and useful when making nets and other rope constructions.

To ensure it doesn't work itself loose, equal strain must be applied to both ends. Create a bight in the rope by doubling it up. Pass this bight around the object you want to tie onto. Pull both ends of the rope through the bight you created, and then pull them both tight.

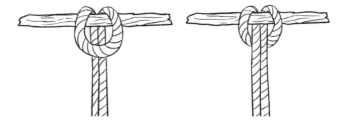

Cow hitch with toggle: This variation is useful when the two ends are secured and only the bight can be passed around the object.

Pass the bight around the object and then put a toggle between the bight and the standing ends to secure it in place.

Reef Knot

A reef knot (a.k.a. square knot) is a good binding knot which is easy to tie and untie.

Many people may use the reef knot to join two ropes together. This is not advised, especially if the rope will be bearing load. There are far better joining knots, which are specifically designed for the job.

To tie a reef knot, put the rope around the object you want to bind. Take the left end, pass it over the right from the bottom, and then tuck it under the right end. Now take this new right end, cross it over the left end, and then tuck it under. Pull the left strands and the right strands apart to tighten the knot.

An easy way to remember this is with the formula "left over right and under, right over left and under."

Surgeon's Knot

A variation of the reef knot is the surgeon's knot, which is more secure.

To tie a surgeon's knot, make an extra turn when tying the "left over right" part. This keeps the knot in place while you tie the rest of the knot. You could also make an extra turn in the "right over left" part to make it even more secure.

Round Turn and Two Half Hitches

This knot is fast to tie and very secure. It's also fairly easy to untie, even when placed under heavy strain.

To create the round turn, loop the running end of the rope around your object so the rope completely encloses it.

Tie a half hitch by bringing the running end behind the standing end. Make a turn around the standing end, and then thread it through the gap you made between the running and standing ends.

Create a second half hitch in the same way, ensuring it's underneath the first half hitch. Pull both ends to tighten.

Timber Hitch

The timber hitch is useful for securing any cylindrical object, such as a wooden log. It's secure when tension is applied, but remains easy to untie even after a heavy load.

It's great for pulling large objects, and is also useful for attaching the string on a longbow, as well as on some instruments, such as guitars.

Loop the rope around the object. Bring the running end under, and then back over, the standing end. Wrap the running end around itself (between the rope and the object) three or four times. Pull it tight.

When using the timber hitch to haul/hoist something, you can add some half hitches towards the hauling end. This will keep the load straight while you pull it.

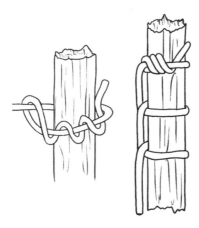

Trucker's Hitch Variation

The trucker's hitch is a simple tension system which is great to use to secure a load on a vehicle, hold down a roof, make a tent guy-line super-tight, etc.

There are a few ways to do a trucker's hitch. This method uses a combination of knots that have already appeared in this book.

Secure one end of the rope (clove hitch, round turn and two half hitches, bow line, etc.) to whatever you are tying the load to. Wrap the running end over the object(s) you wish to secure, and then back down.

Create a fixed loop, such as a butterfly loop. about two thirds up this line. Pass the running end under a secure point and then back up through the fixed loop you made.

Pull down as much as possible to tighten the load down, and then tie the rope off on itself with a couple of half hitches.

Related Chapters:

- Lashing
- Loops
- Knot Tying Terms

BENDS

Bends are used to join two or more lengths of rope together. They can be useful in repairing broken rope or for creating a longer length from two shorter ones.

Figure-Eight Bend

The figure-eight bend is a fairly easy and secure way to join two ropes together. It's also good for making a prusik loop of rope, which can be used for ascending. It's best done with ropes of equal width, especially if it will hold a critical load.

Tie a loose figure-eight in the end of one of the ropes. Follow the path of the original figure-eight with the other rope, much as you would with a threaded figure-eight). Ensure that there's no crossover in the rope and that the ends face in opposite directions. Pull on all ends to tighten them.

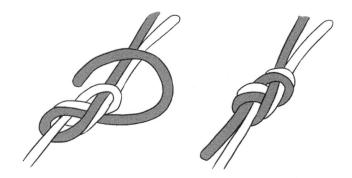

Sheet Bend

The sheet bend is a fast way to join two ropes together.

Create a bight in one of the ropes. Pass the running end of the second rope through the bight, so that it loops over the top of the first rope and under itself. Tighten the bend by pulling both ends of the first rope away from the standing end of the second rope.

Double Sheet Bend

The double sheet bend can be used when you want more security, such as when strain on the rope will be intermittent, when the rope is wet, and/or when the ropes you're using are of a different thickness.

Making a double sheet bend is the same as making a normal sheet bend, except that you loop the second rope around the first one a second time before tucking it under itself.

When using ropes of a different thickness, have the thinner rope be the second one.

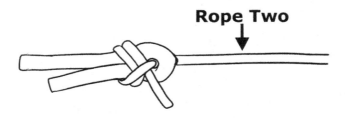

Related Chapters:

- Loops
- Ascending

LASHING

Lashing is used to join objects together. It becomes very useful during construction. You will need to have quite a long running end for all lashings.

Square Lashing

Square lashing is used to hold poles together at a 90° angle.

Place two poles together in a cross, so that the vertical one is on top of the horizontal one. Tie a clove hitch on the vertical pole, below the horizontal one. Pass the running end under the horizontal pole (on the right side of the vertical pole), then over the vertical one (on the upper side of the horizontal pole). Then pass the running end under the horizontal pole on the left side, and pull it tight, so that the clove hitch slips to the right side of the vertical pole.

Continue to pass the rope over the verticals and then under the horizontals, moving counterclockwise. Pull each pass tight as you go. Make three full rotations.

The long end of the rope should end up underneath the right side of the horizontal pole. Bring it back over the front of the horizontal pole, and then behind the lower end of the vertical pole. This is called frapping. Pull it tight.

Go over the left side of the horizontal pole and then under the top side of the vertical one, and pull the rope tight. This is one frapping rotation. Do a total of three frapping rotations and then tie a clove hitch on the lower side of the vertical pole.

When doing the clove hitch, make sure you pull the first half hitch tight before doing the second.

Trim any excess away and/or tuck it under the lashing.

Diagonal Lashing

Diagonal lashing can be used when the poles don't cross at right angles. It's also useful when the poles need to be pulled toward each other for tying.

Cross two poles on top of each other and tie a surgeon's knot around them horizontally, so that the running end is to the right. Pass the running end back behind the poles, so it's on the left side. Bring the running end horizontally over and under the poles. Pull it tight. Do this three times.

The running end should finish on the left. Go over the bottom left pole and then under the cross, so it comes over the top vertically. Pull it tight.

Do three vertical turns and pull tight after each one. Your running end should finish running down.

Do some frapping turns by passing the rope under and then over each pole counterclockwise. Keep it tight. Do three full rotations.

Finish it off with a clove hitch and trim it if needed.

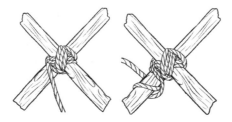

Sheer Lashing

A sheer lashing is good for joining poles together in a parallel fashion.

Put two poles together side by side so they lie horizontally. Tie one clove hitch around both the poles, to the left of where you intend to make the rest of the lashing.

Lay the short end horizontally between the two poles to the right of your clove hitch, so that you will lash over them. Wrap the running end around the two poles, pulling it tight after each turn. Do enough turns to ensure that the lashing is the same length as the width of the two poles.

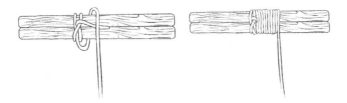

Do frapping turns by passing the rope between the two poles on the right side and then coming back up between them on the left. This should be hard to do since you pulled the lashing turns tightly.

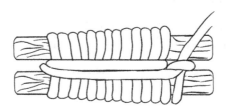

Do two frapping turns and finish with a clove hitch around one end one of the poles.

Note: You can place wedges in between the two poles instead of frapping.

A-frame Lashing

An A-frame lashing is the same as a sheer one, but with looser lashing and frapping turns. Pull the legs apart to make the A-frame.

SURVIVAL ROPING TECHNIQUES

The methods described in these bonus chapters make use of some of the knots described in the main part of this book. These are techniques which you may find useful when in a survival situation.

Warning: The following techniques are reserved for "no-other-option" survival situations. If you choose to practice them ensure you take all the necessary precautions and care to ensure your safety.

The following information is from the book *Emergency Roping and Bouldering* by Sam Fury.

www.SurvivalFitnessPlan.com/Emergency-Roping

DESCENDING

The technique for rappelling with only a rope is known as the Dulfersitz method.

For this to work, you need a rope that's at least twice the length of the distance you wish to descend and that's strong enough to hold your weight.

Find the middle of the rope and wrap it around a solid anchor. Ensure it's not rubbing against any sharp edges and test its stability with all your weight. Jerk on it to make sure.

Pass both ends of the rope between your legs from front to back, and then to the left of your body, over your right shoulder, and down your back.

For comfort (and if you have the resources) you can put some padding around your shoulders and groin.

Hold the rope in front with your left hand and at the back with your right.

Plant your feet firmly against the slope about 45cm apart, and lean back so that the rope supports your weight. Do not try to hold yourself up with your hands.

Step slowly downwards while lowering your hands one at a time.

ASCENDING

Prusiking up a rope is a self-rescue method used by climbers. It's a relatively safe way to ascend a rope when there is no easy way to climb out. It can also be used in reverse if you need to descend.

Climbers will have proper equipment such as harnesses and carabineers, but chances are you will not. Still, prusiking up a rope without a harness is safer than trying to ascend without using a prusik system. Improvised harnesses, or even just a short rope tied around the waist using a bowline, can (and should) also be made if you have enough resources to do so.

The first thing you must do is create two closed loops. These will be your prusik loops. Many types of knots can be used to create a closed loop, but most of them are not safe to use when prusiking.

Climbers often use a double fisherman's knot, but a faster way is to use a figure-eight bend. This type of bend knot is also easier to tie than a double fisherman's and easier to untie, even after your weight has been on it.

Your two prusik loops should be made from rope about half the diameter of the rope you are going to ascend or descend. Ideally, one rope will be about 20cm longer than you are tall, and the second rope will be twice your height.

The rope you use for your prusik loops must strong enough to hold you if you fall. This doesn't just mean it can hold your weight; it has to be strong enough to handle the shock load.

Prusik Hitch

Once you've made your prusik loops, you'll use the prusik hitch to attach them to the rope you want to climb (the main line).

Put the loop across your main line, with the joining knot (figure-eight bend) facing the right. Wrap your prusik loop around the main line on the knotted side. Do this at least twice. The more wraps you make, the more friction you'll have.

Slowly tighten the loops As you do so, ensure all the lines are neatly next to each other. Do not let them overlap or cross each other. As you tighten the loops, do your best to position the figure-eight bend close to the main line.

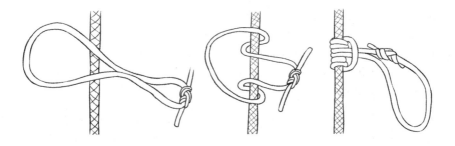

Ascending the Main Line Using Prusik Loops

Tie both prusik loops onto the main line using prusik hitches. Tie the smaller prusik loop above the larger one.

A prusik hitch works because you can slide it up, but it doesn't slip when downward tension is applied. Test it well with all your weight before using it to climb. Add extra turns if needed.

Attach the top prusik loop to your harness.

Note: Rope-on-rope friction can cut rope. If you have a carabiner, use it. If not, just be extra careful there's not too much friction between your harness and the prusik loop.

Slide the top prusik loop up as high as you can reach.

Slide the bottom prusik loop to about head height, or as high as you can get it and still put your foot in it. Put your foot in the loop and stand up. The joining knot of the prusik loop is the weak part, so keep off it.

Slide the top prusik loop as high as possible, and then put your weight on it by sitting in your harness. Now slide your bottom prusik loop up as high as possible and put your foot in it. Stand up and slide the top prusik loop up again. Repeat this motion.

To descend, just reverse the motions.

Ascending Without a Harness

It is possible to ascend using prusik loops with no harness, but doing so is extremely risky and uses considerably more energy. Sufficient strength is needed.

Make your loops smaller than usual and have at least two of them, preferably four.

Assuming you're using four prusik loops, the top two are for your hands and the bottom two are for your feet. You want them all to be fairly snug so you can slide them up with minimal movement.

Place your feet in the two bottom prusik loops and hold on to the top ones with your hands. Slide your hands up with the top prusik loops as high as you can. Pull yourself up and use your legs to slide the bottom prusik loops up as high as you can, then stand up while sliding the top prusik loops up again. Repeat this process.

Brake and Squat

If you don't have any rope to use as prusik loops, you can use the brake-and-squat method to climb the rope.

Let the rope fall to the outside of one of your legs. Step on the rope with the foot closest to it, then put your other foot underneath it. You're now in the basic position.

Grab the rope as high up as possible and hang off it. Bring your feet up as high as possible (pull yourself up and bring your knees to your chest) and place them in the basic position. This position locks the rope in so you can stand (and rest if needed). Reach up as high as you can again and repeat the process.

Ladder of Knots

A series of overhand knots tied at intervals along a smooth rope will make climbing much easier.

Rope Ladder

One way to make a rope ladder is to tie as many fixed loops (butterfly loops work well) in a rope as you need hand- and footholds.

Another way is by using two ropes (or one rope doubled up). Tie fixed loops opposite each other along the ropes. As you do so, put sticks (the rungs of the ladder) in the loops and slowly tighten the knot around them to hold them in place. Allow the rung ends to protrude out the sides of the knots a bit so they won't slip out.

Related Chapters:

- Loops
- Hitches
- Improvised Harnesses

IMPROVISED HARNESSES

Improvised rope harnesses may not be that comfortable, but they are very useful to know how to make.

Triple Bowline

A triple bowline is basically a bowline made with a doubled-up line.

It produces three loops which can be used (among other things) as a sit sling or a lifting harness, with one loop around each thigh and the other around the chest.

Tie it in the exact same way as a bowline, using the middle of the rope. Do not use the ends. The running end must protrude out far enough to create the third loop.

When using this to haul people, be careful of the pressure the rope may create on the chest. A foot loop can be made to release the pressure.

Swiss Seat

This is an improvised harness that's good enough to use when doing things such as using prusik loops for ascension, assuming you don't have a commercial harness.

Find the center of the rope. Loop it around your waist and tie the first half of a surgeon's knot at your front.

Pass the ends between your legs and then tuck them up through the wrap you made around your waist, on either side of your waist.

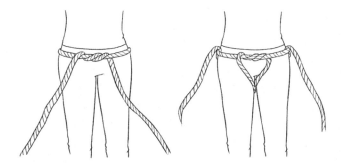

Pull down on the ends as you do a few squats. This will tighten it as well as check for comfort. Next, do a full wrap around your "belt" with each end of the rope.

Tie the ends together using a reef knot. Do it a little off center to make room for a carabiner. Make half hitches with the leftover rope that goes around both "belts."

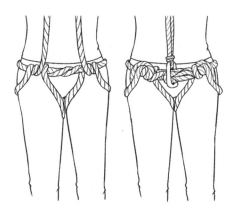

Related Chapters:

- Loops
- Hitches

SELF-RESCUE BOWLINE

The self-rescue bowline is good to learn in case you find yourself in a "man overboard" situation or something similar. It is tying a bowline around your waist with only one hand.

Wrap the rope around your waist so that both the standing and running ends are to your front, with your body (waist) between them. In this demonstration, the running end is on your right.

Hold the running end in your right, hand allowing at least 15cm of rope beyond your hand. Without letting go of the running end, bring it over the standing part to make a crossing point.

Bring it up though the gap created between your body and the crossing point. The rope will be wrapped around your hand.

Using your fingers, but without letting go of the rope, pass the running end under the standing part, just beyond the first crossing point. This creates a second crossing point.

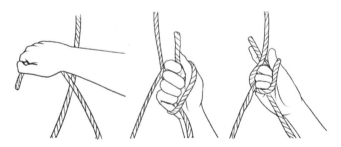

Continue to maneuver the running end with your fingers so that it feeds between the two crossing points. It feeds from the top down. You should end up holding the running end.

Once that's accomplished, pull your hand out from the loop on your wrist, bringing the running end with you. Pull the knot tight.

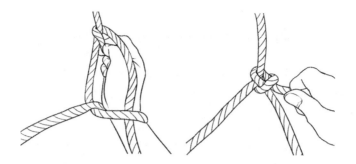

RIVER CROSSING WITH ROPE

In a survival situation, crossing a river can be an extremely risky venture. Using this method will reduce a lot of the risk, although it will still be dangerous.

You need at least three people and a rope three times the width of the river.

The first and last people to cross should be the strongest in the group, with the stronger of the two going first.

Tie the rope into a large loop and secure the person who is going to cross first (person A) to the loop. Tie a butterfly loop in the rope and put it over his/her chest.

As person A crosses, the other two let the rope out as needed. They must do their best to keep the rope out of the water, and be ready to haul person A back if needed.

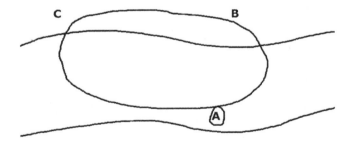

Person A is the only one secured to the rope.

When person A reaches the other side, he/she unties him-/herself.

As many people as needed can now cross (B), one at a time, by securing themselves to the rope and crossing over.

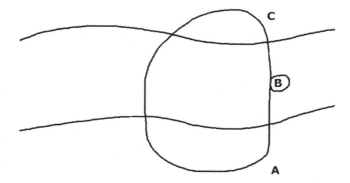

Although multiple people can help while others are crossing, the strongest person (A) should take most of the strain by being as close to directly across from the person crossing as possible.

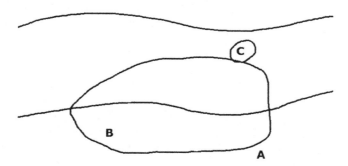

MAKING A GILL NET

A gill net is time- and resource-intensive to construct, but is very effective at catching marine life or birds when you're in a survival situation.

Tie a suspension line between two trees for you to work off. Get many lengths of cord and tie them to the suspension line using cow hitches. Space them about 10cm apart. Tie the separate lines together using overhand knots. Space them vertically, about 10cm apart.

Another line can be tied between the trees as a guideline. Use the guideline to ensure you tie the joining overhand knots at the same height.

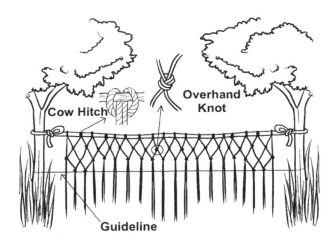

Once you're finished, you can attach floats at the top and weights at the bottom. This will keep the net vertical in the water.

Stretch the gill net across a river. It will be most effective in still water, such as a lake (near the inlet and outlet are good locations) or in the backwater of a large stream.

The gill net will catch everything, so don't deploy it for very long.

When in the open sea, pass a gill net under the keel of your raft or boat from end to end. It will catch whatever is attracted to the shelter created by your craft.

MAKING ROPE

Rope (cord, string, etc.) is extremely useful and can be improvised from many different materials, including fabric, fishing line, and shoelaces.

When there is no such thing available (or you're not willing to sacrifice it), then other common materials can be made into rope. Suitable ones include:

- Animal hair.
- Inner bark (cedar, chestnut, elm, hickory, linden, mulberry, and white oak work well). Shred the plant fibers from the inner bark.
- Fibrous stems (honeysuckle and stinging nettles work well).
- Grasses.
- Palms.
- Rushes.
- Sinew (dry tendons of large game).
- Rawhide.
- Vines (strong vines can be used without any other preparation, but plant fibers spun together will be more durable).

Making Rope from Plant Material

When you think you have a suitable plant material, see if it can withstand the following tests.

Note: Stiff fibers can be softened by steaming them or soaking them in water.

- Pull the ends in opposite directions.
- Twist and roll it between your fingers.
- Tie an overhand knot in it.

To turn the material into rope, twine it together. Collect a small pile of it. Divide it in half and rotate one half before recombining them. This ensures an even consistency in your rope.

Get a bunch of the material, depending on how thick you want your cordage/rope, and knot it together at one end.

Divide the remaining side of the bundle into two even sections and twist them both clockwise to create two strands.

Next, twist one of the strands around the other counterclockwise. Tie the end to prevent it from unraveling.

You can join shorter lengths together by splicing them. Do so by twisting the ends of their strands together while they're still in two lengths, before the counterclockwise twisting. Twist one small bunch on each side (for each of the strands) and then just continue to twist as before. You can do this as much as you want until you get the desired length of rope.

Thicker ropes can be made by using larger bundles of grass or by twisting multiple ropes together.

Making Rope from Animals

In a survival situation, you may be fortunate enough to capture game. Waste nothing.

Sinew is an excellent material for small lashings. Remove the tendons from game animals and dry them. Once they're completely dry, hammer them until they are fibrous. Add some moisture so you can twist the fibers together. You could also braid them together, which would make a stronger product.

Sinew is sticky when wet and hardens when dry. You can lash small items together while the sinew is wet, and since it dries hard, the actual use of knots is not necessary.

When the job is too big for sinew, rawhide can be used. Skin any medium to large game and clean the skin very well. Make sure there's no fat or meat, though hair/fur is okay. Dry it completely. If there are folds that will capture moisture, you'll need to stretch the skin out. Once it's dry, cut it into a continuous 5mm- to 10mm-wide length. The best way to do this is to begin in the middle of the skin and cut outwards in circles, expanding the spiral as you go.

To use the rawhide, soak it until it's soft. This usually takes two to four hours. Use it wet and stretch it as much as you can as you do so. Leave to dry.

Related Chapters:

- Lashing

THROWING ROPE

Knowing how to throw rope properly will greatly increase the distance you can throw it. In most cases, you should aim to throw it further than you think you need to. If you intend to keep one end of the rope (which is usually the case), be sure to secure it to something.

Note: Even when throwing all the rope to someone, it's a good idea to secure one end. If your throw doesn't clear the obstacle, you can pull the rope back, and if it does, you can just untie the rope and your friend can pull it over.

Tie a weight or several overhand knots to the end you're going to throw over. Coil half the rope in the palm of your right hand. Coil the rest of it on your fingers.

Stand on one end to secure it, or tie it to something. Grab the coils you made on your fingers with your left hand.

As you throw, release the right-hand coils a split second before the left. When throwing a weighted rope over a branch, beware of it swinging back.

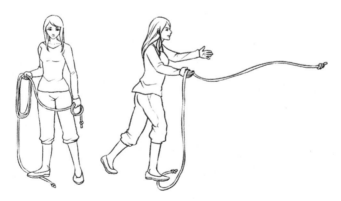

THANKS FOR READING

Dear reader,

Thank you for reading *The Useful Knots Book*.

If you enjoyed this book, please leave a review where you bought it. It helps more than most people think.

Don't forget your FREE book chapters!

You will also be among the first to know of FREE review copies, discount offers, bonus content, and more.

Go to:

https://offers.SFNonfictionBooks.com/Free-Chapters

Thanks again for your support.

REFERENCES

Brayak, D. Keenan, T. (2007). *Coopers Rock Bouldering Guide (Bouldering Series)*. Falcon Guides.

Budworth, G. Dalton, J. (2016). The Little Book of Incredibly Useful Knots: 200 Practical Knots for Sailors, Climbers, Campers & Other Adventurers. Skyhorse.

Emerson, C. (2016). *100 Deadly Skills: Survival Edition*. Atria Books.

Hanson, J. (2015). *Spy Secrets That Can Save Your Life*. TarcherPerigee.

Hanson, J. (2018). *Survive Like a Spy*. TarcherPerigee.

Jarmin, C. (2013). *The Knot Tying Bible: Climbing, Camping, Sailing, Fishing, Everyday*. Firefly Books.

Jäger, J. Sundsten, B. (2014). *My First Book of Knots: A Beginner's Picture Guide (180 color illustrations)*. Sky Pony.

Wiseman, J. (2015). *SAS Survival Guide*. William Collins.

AUTHOR RECOMMENDATIONS

Teach Yourself Evasive Wilderness Survival

Discover all the evasive survival skills you need, because if you can survive under these circumstances, you can survive anything.

Get it now.

www.SFNonfictionBooks.com/Evasive-Wilderness-Survival-Techniques

This is the Only Wilderness Medicine Book You Need

Discover what you need to heal yourself, because a little knowledge goes a long way.

Get it now.

www.SFNonfictionBooks.com/Wilderness-Travel-Medicine

ABOUT SAM FURY

Sam Fury has had a passion for survival, evasion, resistance, and escape (SERE) training since he was a young boy growing up in Australia.

This led him to years of training and career experience in related subjects, including martial arts, military training, survival skills, outdoor sports, and sustainable living.

These days, Sam spends his time refining existing skills, gaining new skills, and sharing what he learns via the Survival Fitness Plan website.

www.SurvivalFitnessPlan.com

amazon.com/author/samfury

goodreads.com/SamFury

facebook.com/AuthorSamFury

instagram.com/AuthorSamFury

youtube.com/SurvivalFitnessPlan

Made in the USA
Coppell, TX
05 November 2022

85826547R00039